ROSEN ✔ *Verified*

U.S. GOVERNMENT

INSIDE THE SUPREME COURT

Jenna Tolli

ROSEN
PUBLISHING

New York

CONTENTS

WHAT IS THE SUPREME COURT?

The Supreme Court is the most powerful court in the United States. It has the power to change decisions made in other courts. The Supreme Court's decisions are considered final. The way the Supreme Court works is based on the U.S. Constitution.

The decisions made in the Supreme Court affect the entire country. The court is made up of nine members called justices. There's one chief justice and eight associate justices. They make hard decisions on many different matters. The Supreme Court has heard many cases. It has made decisions about presidential elections, health care, civil rights, marriage, and many other issues.

The court meets in the Supreme Court building in Washington, D.C.

HISTORY OF THE COURT

The U.S. Constitution was written and signed in 1787. It explains the way the government is set up. It helps protect the rights of citizens. The Constitution also outlines the way the justice system is supposed to work.

Article III, Section 1 of the Constitution explains that the country is to have a Supreme Court. It gives details about how the Supreme Court is set up. For example, it explains that there are many lower courts in the United States and one Supreme Court.

FAST FACT
THE SUPREME COURT BUILDING IN WASHINGTON, D.C., IS OPEN TO THE PUBLIC! VISITORS CAN WALK THROUGH CERTAIN PARTS OF THE BUILDING AND EVEN HEAR ARGUMENTS IN REAL CASES.

Article III of the Constitution outlines how the **judicial** system works.

HOW THE COURT WORKS

The Supreme Court works differently from the way you might usually think a court works. It doesn't call witnesses to hear their side of the story. It doesn't have a jury to decide whether or not someone is guilty.

Instead, the Supreme Court usually reviews appeals. These are reviews of decisions from cases that have already been tried in other courts. The Supreme Court reads the records from the other cases to help make its decision. It can also hear some cases for the first time, but this isn't as common.

STRAIGHT TO THE TOP

When the Supreme Court is the only court to hear a case, it's called original **jurisdiction**. This happens when there is a disagreement between states or foreign **representatives**.

In the first 170 years of the Supreme Court (1789 to 1959), it heard only 123 original jurisdiction cases.

LOWER-LEVEL COURTS

The Supreme Court is the last stop for a case. Two lower courts see most cases first. District courts are where most **federal** trials are held for the first time. A judge and sometimes a jury make the decision on a case after they hear facts and **evidence**.

The losing side of a case can ask for an appeal. This is a review of the lower court's decision. U.S. courts of appeals look at the decisions from district courts. They decide if the law was applied correctly.

Someone can file an appeal if they think there was a mistake in their case. There must be a legal, or law-related, reason.

THREE LEVELS OF FEDERAL COURT

U.S. SUPREME COURT
1 court

U.S. COURTS OF APPEALS
13 courts

U.S. DISTRICT COURTS
94 courts

IMPORTANCE OF THE SUPREME COURT

The Constitution was written more than 200 years ago. Many of the issues the country faces today are different. Part of the Supreme Court's job is to **interpret** the Constitution. Its decisions help make modern laws.

The Supreme Court is the highest court in the land. Its rulings are the final decision on a case. There are no other options for a case after it's been heard by the Supreme Court.

The words "equal justice under law" are engraved on the Supreme Court building. The court makes sure the law is fair to all citizens.

EQUAL·JUSTICE·UNDER·LAW·

13

HOW DOES A CASE GET TO THE SUPREME COURT?

Sometimes, people aren't happy with the result of their first appeal. They may then ask the Supreme Court to hear their case. The justices and their staff review a list of requests. They decide whether to accept a case. At least four of the nine justices need to agree. If they do, the case is accepted.

The Supreme Court chooses its cases very carefully. It's asked to review thousands of cases every year. It agrees to hear only about 80 cases each year.

FAST FACT

THE LOSER OF A CASE CAN ASK THE SUPREME COURT TO GRANT A WRIT OF CERTIORARI. THIS IS A LEGAL ORDER FROM THE SUPREME COURT TO ASK FOR CASE RECORDS FROM A LOWER COURT.

What happens to the thousands of cases that don't get picked? It doesn't mean the Supreme Court agrees or disagrees with the case. It just means the decision from the lower court will stand.

INSIDE THE SUPREME COURT

The Supreme Court is free to accept or turn down cases. It doesn't have to follow a set of rules. However, there are some common reasons why it agrees to hear a case. Three of the common ones are:

1. If the case affects the whole country or has national **significance**.

2. If a lower court's decision is different from federal law or a past decision.

3. If a court in one part of the country makes a decision that's different from one made in another part of the country.

The Supreme Court was involved in the U.S. presidential election in 2000. The votes in this race were very close. The court had to decide whether they should be recounted. This case impacted the whole country.

San Antonio Express-News

Serving South Texas since 1865

day, November 8, 2000

State Edition 50¢

	Electoral votes	Popular vote	All figures as of 11:36 p.m.
BUSH	246	49%	38,056,069
GORE	242	48%	37,419,188

WHAT A RACE!

History-making presidential election still too close to call

By Gary M

Wednesday

Olympics
Voters support bid for Games
Page 29A

• Election results as compiled by the offices of the secretary of state and the Harris County clerk: **Page 40A.**

ELECTION 2000
12-page special section, Pages 29A-40A

• Latest results can also be found online at www.houstonchronicle.com/election

Legislature
GOP scores key state Senate win
Page 29A

Houston Chronicle

Wednesday, Nov. 8, 2000

Vol. 100 No. 26

50 ¢

Gore, Bush in cliffhang

Battle for White House seesaws through r

By BENNETT ROTH
Houston Chronicle

WASHINGTON —
Gore waited nervously
turns suggested their
White House remained

While Bush, the gov
ing the South and Ro
President Gore was n
Northeast and Califo

Neither
toral Co
the poll

A spec
television
the evening based
back into the und

FAST FACT
THE SUPREME COURT ISN'T REQUIRED TO HEAR SPECIFIC CASES. EVEN IF THE CASE HAS TO DO WITH ONE OF THESE ISSUES, THE COURT MIGHT NOT ACCEPT IT.

17

ORAL ARGUMENTS

The Supreme Court term starts in October. The justices hear cases from October to April. Cases are usually heard early in the week. The justices hear two cases a day. Each one lasts about an hour.

During this time, lawyers from each side have 30 minutes to talk about their case. This is called an oral argument. The justices have already read the records and details about the case beforehand. The justices spend time asking questions during oral arguments.

FAST FACT

LAW CLERKS ARE RECENT LAW SCHOOL GRADUATES WHO WORK FOR THE JUSTICES. THEY HELP DO RESEARCH, THINK OF QUESTIONS, AND WRITE SUMMARIES OF CASES AND REQUESTS. EACH JUSTICE HAS THREE OR FOUR LAW CLERKS EACH TERM.

Just like other judges, Supreme Court justices often talk about cases with their law clerks to get different **perspectives**. They also research decisions from past cases.

HOW ARE DECISIONS MADE?

After they hear a case, the justices need to make their ruling. This is done at a meeting called the Justices' Conference. This meeting happens on Wednesdays and Fridays when the court is in session.

No one other than the justices is allowed in the room during the conference. They discuss the cases they heard and give their decisions. The justices talk about their point of view. At these meetings, they also decide which future cases they will accept.

Everything said by the justices during these conferences is kept completely **confidential**. Only their final decisions are made public.

THE FINAL DECISION

The Supreme Court needs a majority to make a final ruling. This means at least five of the nine members must agree. The closest a ruling can be is 5–4. This means five justices agreed and four didn't. In the last two decades, this has happened in 19 percent of cases.

A unanimous decision means all the justices agreed after hearing a case. Justices have all agreed a lot in the last 20 years. Unanimous decisions have happened about 36 percent of the time.

WORTH THE WAIT

The Supreme Court doesn't make an immediate decision on cases. It can take up to nine months to announce a ruling. A lot of thought and research goes into each vote.

Washington Star-News

Yield Tapes, Nixon Ordered In 8 to 0 High Court Decision

"...To ensure that justice is done"

Hogan May Quit Md. Race Under Fire on Nixon Issue

Trend Quickens To Impeachment

Impeach

Athens Celeb New Civil

In 1974, the Supreme Court unanimously ruled that the president is not above the law. It ordered President Nixon to provide audiotapes during impeachment hearings.

OPINIONS OF THE COURT

After the court makes a decision, the justices announce it to the public. This is done by writing opinions. These are the official rulings of the court. Opinions explain the background and legal reasons why the justices made that decision.

✓ VERIFIED

The first version of the court's opinion on a case is called a slip opinion. These can be found on the court's website:
www.supremecourt.gov/opinions/slipopinion

(Slip Opinion)　　　OCTOBER TERM, 2009　　　　1

Syllabus

NOTE: Where it is feasible, a syllabus (headnote) will be released, as is being done in connection with this case, at the time the opinion is issued. The syllabus constitutes no part of the opinion of the Court but has been prepared by the Reporter of Decisions for the convenience of the reader. See *United States* v. *Detroit Timber & Lumber Co.,* 200 U. S. 321, 337.

SUPREME COURT OF THE UNITED STATES

Syllabus

ALABAMA ET AL. *v.* NORTH CAROLINA

ON EXCEPTIONS TO THE PRELIMINARY AND SECOND REPORTS
OF THE SPECIAL MASTER

No. 132, Orig.　Argued January 11, 2010　Decided June 1, 2010

In 1986, Congress granted its consent to the Southeast Interstate Low-

When all of the Supreme Court's written opinions are published for the term, they can be thousands of pages long!

...entif[y] a host State for the development of a [new] regional-disposal facility," and to "seek to ensure that such facility is license[d] and ready to operate ... no ... later than 1991." Art. 4(E)(6)...

One of the justices who agrees with the majority is chosen to write the opinion of the court. The opinions are released in printed pamphlets, or booklets. They're given out at the court's public information office. They're also posted online. The government collects opinions and releases a book of them each year.

DISSENT

At least one justice often disagrees with the majority. They can write a dissenting opinion to explain their thoughts on the case. To dissent means to disagree with an official decision. Dissenting opinions allow justices who disagree to have their voices heard. It also gives future courts a way to look back on cases and see what went into different decisions.

Justices can also write an opinion if they agree with the final decision but not the reasons behind it. This is called a concurring opinion. To concur means to agree.

DISSENT FOR GOOD

In the 1896 *Plessy v. Ferguson* case, the Supreme Court upheld a racial segregation law. Justice John Marshall Harlan was the only one to disagree with the majority. His dissent supported civil rights and was used decades later when the decision was overturned.

In some cases, one dissent can change the opinion of the court. Justice Ruth Bader Ginsburg has discussed the importance of writing a dissenting opinion.

HOW JUSTICES ARE CHOSEN

There can be only nine Supreme Court justices at a time. New justices join only when a member retires or dies.

The Constitution includes instructions for how to add new members to the Supreme Court. First, the president **nominates** someone. Then, the Senate must give its official approval.

This system gets all branches of government involved. This includes the executive branch (the president) and the legislative branch (Congress).

A presidential nomination doesn't always lead to a hearing. Hearings for one of President Obama's nominees, Merrick Garland, didn't move forward.

THREE BRANCHES OF GOVERNMENT

LEGISLATIVE BRANCH
makes laws

- CONGRESS
  - SENATE
  - HOUSE OF REPRESENTATIVES

EXECUTIVE BRANCH
carries out laws

- PRESIDENT
  - VICE PRESIDENT
  - CABINET

JUDICIAL BRANCH
interprets laws

- SUPREME COURT
  - OTHER FEDERAL COURTS

FAST FACT

GEORGE WASHINGTON CHOSE ALL THE MEMBERS OF THE FIRST SUPREME COURT SINCE HE WAS THE FIRST PRESIDENT.

CONFIRMATION HEARINGS

The Senate Judiciary Committee is a group of 22 senators. After a Supreme Court nomination is made, they hold a **confirmation** hearing.

At the hearing, they collect information about the nominee. They also ask for the nominee's thoughts on some issues. This helps them understand how the nominee might vote on future cases. After the hearing, the Senate holds a vote. This vote decides whether the nominee is confirmed or rejected.

CLOSEST CONFIRMATION VOTES FOR SUPREME COURT JUSTICES

Justice	Vote
Brett Kavanaugh (2018)	51.02%
Stanley Matthews (1881)	51.06%
Clarence Thomas (1991)	52.00%
Nathan Clifford (1958)	53.06%
Lucius Lamar (1888)	53.33%
Neil M. Gorsuch (1991)	54.55%

President Donald Trump's Supreme Court nominations, Brett Kavanaugh and Neil Gorsuch, were barely confirmed. However, they both made the cut.

On average, it takes about 67 days to reach the Senate's final vote after the president nominates a Supreme Court justice.

rk Times

National Edition

New Mexico: Cloudy to par
sunny. A few showers north. Afte
noon thunderstorms southwes
Highs in the upper 50s to the middl
80s. Weather map is on Page 22

Printed in New Mexico $6.00

2018

SENATE VOTES 50-48 TO PUT KAVANAUGH ON SUPREME COURT

Confirmation Battle May Have Eroded the Public Trust

By ADAM LIPTAK

WASHINGTON — For Presi-
dent Trump and for Senate Re-
publicans, confirming Judge Brett
M. Kavanaugh as a Supreme
Court justice was a hard-won political victory. But for the conservative legal movement, it is a signal
triumph, the culmination of a dec-
ades-long project that began in
the Reagan era with the

Judge Is Sworn In, Tilting Ideological Balance to Right

By SHERYL GAY STOLBERG

WASHINGTON — Judge Bret
M. Kavanaugh was confirmed t
the Supreme Court on Saturda
by one of the slimmest margins i
American history, locking in a so
solid conservative majority

WHO CAN BE ON THE SUPREME COURT?

The Constitution doesn't give rules for who can join the Supreme Court. There is no age limit. Justices don't have to hold a certain degree. They don't even have to have certain kinds of experience. Still, all justices have been trained in the law. They always have legal backgrounds.

There is no citizenship requirement to be on the Supreme Court. This means someone born in another country can become a justice. As of 2020, six justices have been born in a foreign country.

NO DEGREE?

Not all justices have held a law degree, but they have all been lawyers. There weren't many law schools in the 1700s and 1800s. This meant some justices worked with **mentors** to study the law.

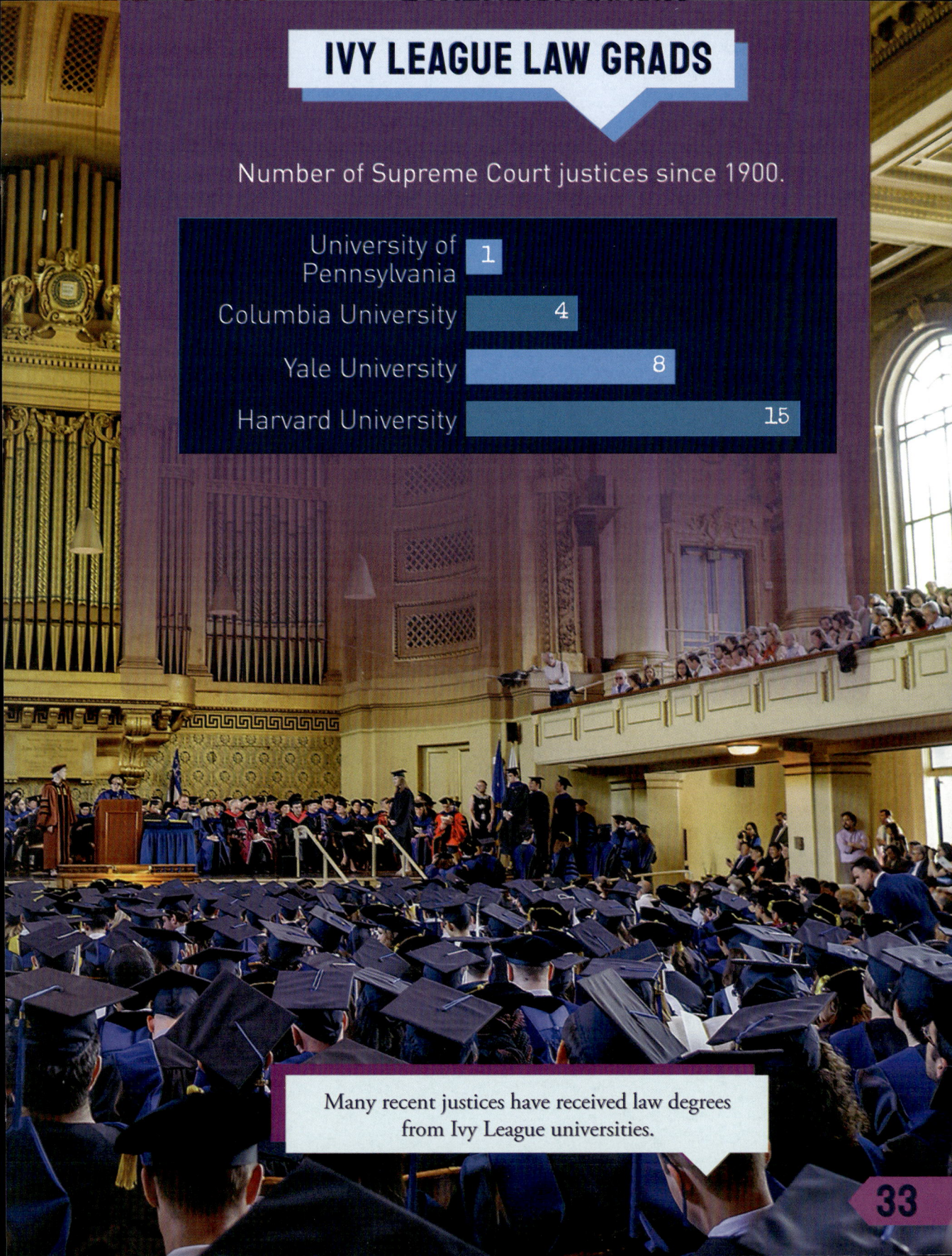

IVY LEAGUE LAW GRADS

Number of Supreme Court justices since 1900.

University of Pennsylvania	1
Columbia University	4
Yale University	8
Harvard University	15

Many recent justices have received law degrees from Ivy League universities.

HOW LONG CAN A JUSTICE SERVE?

Supreme Court justices may serve on the court for a long time. Most stay until they retire. Others have **resigned**. Some have stayed until they died. The only other way a justice would leave the court is if they were impeached and removed.

You may have heard about impeachment for presidents. If Congress thinks the president committed a crime, it can bringing charges against the president. This is called impeachment. Federal court judges can also be impeached. This includes members of the Supreme Court.

✓ **VERIFIED**

You can learn more about how the impeachment process works on the Senate's website: https://www.senate.gov/reference/Index/Impeachment.htm

Impeachment is rare in the U.S. government. Only three presidents have been impeached. Only one Supreme Court justice has been impeached.

COURT DIVERSITY

Diversity is part of U.S. history. It's important to have diversity on our courts too. From 1790 until 1967, all Supreme Court justices were white men. Thurgood Marshall was the court's first black justice. He joined the court in 1967.

Sandra Day O'Connor was the first female justice. She joined the court in 1981. There have been only three other women on the court. They are Ruth Bader Ginsburg, Sonia Sotomayor, and Elena Kagan. All three were on the court as of 2020. Sonia Sotomayor is also the first Hispanic justice.

When a new justice joins the court, it's a tradition for all members of the Supreme Court to take a new group photo.

JUSTICES AS OF 2019

The Supreme Court members in this photo are: Associate Justice Stephen Breyer, Associate Justice Clarence Thomas, Chief Justice John Roberts, Associate Justice Ruth Bader Ginsburg, Associate Justice Samuel Alito Jr., Associate Justice Neil Gorsuch, Associate Justice Sonia Sotomayor, Associate Justice Elena Kagan, and Associate Justice Brett Kavanaugh.

HOW THE SUPREME COURT AFFECTS US

Court cases always affect the people involved. This is true whether they win or lose. Cases that reach the Supreme Court can affect the entire country. The justices have the power to interpret the Constitution. Their rulings give answers to important questions.

Some decisions can change the everyday lives of Americans. Some Supreme Court cases make history and affect the nation for decades. These are called landmark cases.

A HEALTHY COURT

In the 2012 case of *National Federation of Independent Business v. Sebelius*, the Supreme Court upheld most parts of the Affordable Care Act. This changed the way some Americans receive health insurance.

People can gather on the sidewalk outside the Supreme Court building to protest or show their support for a case. Crowds often gather during **controversial** cases.

LANDMARK CASES

The Supreme Court has decided many landmark cases over the past 200 years. It's made rulings that affect students' rights, presidential elections, how Americans receive health care, and more.

Obergefell v. Hodges was a landmark 2015 case. The Supreme Court ruled that the Constitution guarantees a right to marriage for same-sex couples.

MAKING LAWS FAIR

In 1954, the Supreme Court ruled in *Brown v. Board of Education* that separating students based on their race was **unconstitutional**. This was a turning point for the civil rights movement.

The court's decisions can also shape future rulings made by lower-level courts. When the Supreme Court makes a ruling, it's used in other cases that involve similar issues. This is called setting a precedent.

FUTURE OF THE SUPREME COURT

The Supreme Court has changed a lot over the years. Justices leave and new ones are appointed. The court looks different with each new appointment. It also makes decisions differently.

Almost every president has been able to nominate justices. President Obama nominated Elena Kagan and Sonia Sotomayor. President Trump nominated Neil Gorsuch and Brett Kavanaugh.

Presidents often choose justices who share their political views. These justices serve for decades. This means the president has a big impact on the court even after he or she leaves office.

In response to a comment from President Trump, Chief Justice Roberts stated:

"We do not have Obama judges or Trump judges . . . What we have is an extraordinary group of dedicated judges doing their level best to do equal right to those appearing before them."

Justices make decisions based on the facts of the case and how it relates to the Constitution. Their decisions shouldn't be based on political influences.

THE LAW OF THE LAND

The Supreme Court has protected the rights of people in the United States for centuries. There will always be more cases and questions to bring to the court. This will be especially true as the country moves forward. The court's rulings are influential, which means they have many effects. That's why it's important that the court remains fair and up to date.

The United States is different now than it was when the Constitution was written. When the Supreme Court decides cases, it still uses the Constitution. The way it interprets that document affects our everyday lives. Modern cases must bring the court's attention to modern issues. As the justices hear these cases, we can hope the U.S. legal system becomes ever more fair and equal.

On average, Supreme Court justices serve for 16 years. Their decisions have lasting impacts on the laws of our country.

GLOSSARY

confidential: Secret or private.

confirmation: The act of giving official approval to someone.

controversial: Likely to give rise to disagreement.

diversity: The quality or state of having many different types, forms, or ideas.

evidence: Something that shows that something else is true.

federal: Relating to the central government of the United States.

interpret: To understand and explain the meaning of something.

judicial: Related to courts or judges.

jurisdiction: The limits or territory within which a person or group can exercise power.

mentor: Someone who teaches, gives guidance, or gives advice to someone, especially a less experienced person.

nominate: To formally choose someone as a candidate for a position.

perspective: Point of view.

representative: A person who acts for someone or something else.

resign: To formally give up a job or position.

significance: Influence or importance.

unconstitutional: Not allowed by the Constitution.

INDEX